LIVEWIRE
YOUTH FICTION

KU-300-811

Little English Girl

Peter Leigh

Published in association with
The Basic Skills Agency

Hodder & Stoughton

Acknowledgements
Illustrations: Stephanie Hawken/Organisation.
Cover: Stephanie Hawken/Organisation.

Orders: please contact Bookpoint Ltd, 39 Milton Park, Abingdon, Oxon OX14
4TD. Telephone: (44) 01235 400414, Fax: (44) 01235 400454. Lines are open
from 9.00–6.00, Monday to Saturday, with a 24 hour message answering service.
Email address: orders@bookpoint.co.uk

British Library Cataloguing in Publication Data
A catalogue record for this title is available from The British Library

ISBN 0 340 72089 1

First published 1998
Impression number   10 9 8 7 6 5 4 3 2
Year   2002 2001 2000 1999

Typeset by Fakenham Photosetting Limited, Fakenham, Norfolk
Printed in Great Britain for Hodder & Stoughton Educational, a division of
Hodder Headline Plc, 338 Euston Road, London NW1 3BH by Athenaeum Press
Ltd, Gateshead, Tyne & Wear.

Little English Girl

Contents

1 Kloppos

The sea was blue,
the sky was clear,
the sun was hot.

And Gemma was bored!

She lay on the beach.
and let the sun toast her.

'This is so boring,'
she said to herself.
'Kloppos is so boring!'

She rolled over,
and looked at the little white town
above the beach.
She could see her hotel,
and the narrow streets winding up
into the mountains.

It was so pretty,
and so peaceful,
and so quiet,
and so boring!

Gemma had not wanted to come to
Kloppos at all. It was her mum and dad.

'Let's go to Kloppos,' they had said.
'It's so peaceful there,
and quiet.'
Peace and quiet!
Gemma did not want peace and quiet.
She wanted discos and beach parties
and windsurfing.
She wanted to spend all day in the sun
and all night in a club.

She wanted to go to Krakkos.
Krakkos was cool!

She knew all about Krakkos.
Her friend Louise had just come back
from there,
and had told them all about it in school.
She told them about how she had been
out all night and nobody minded,
and about how she had drunk iced champagne,
and about how this boy
wanted to go for a midnight swim with her.

Then she had gathered all the girls
around her,
and pulled down the shoulder of her T-shirt
to show off her tan.

There were no strap marks!

Gemma wanted a tan with no strap marks.
And she wanted to drink iced champagne.
And she wanted to go for a midnight swim
with a boy.

But there was no chance for any of
those things in Kloppos,
nor for discos or beach-parties
or windsurfing.

Not with her mum and dad.

She had tried to get them to go to Krakkos
instead, and had nearly won,
because for a few weeks
Kloppos had been on the TV every night.
It was big news –
something about fighting in the mountains.

'See,' said Gemma.
'There's no peace and quiet in Kloppos.
Let's go to Krakkos instead.'

But then the fighting had died down.
'It was nothing to worry about,' said her dad.
'We'll still go to Kloppos.'

He was right.
Everything was peaceful and quiet.
There had been some tanks outside the airport
which had shocked Gemma,
and once a lorry full of soldiers
had pulled into the square behind the hotel.
They had green uniforms, and dark glasses,
and guns at their hips.

There had been a lot of shouting.
Gemma thought she heard a shot,
and some men had got in the back of the lorry
with the soldiers.

But then they had driven off,
and everything was quiet again.

Gemma rolled over once more.
'This is so boring!'
she said again.

She heard her dad calling for her
from the hotel.
It was time for dinner.
She sighed, stood up,
and wrapped her towel round her.

'Kloppos is the most boring place
in the world,' she said to herself as she
walked across the beach to the hotel.
But Gemma was wrong.
She would not be bored in Kloppos
for much longer!

2 Istvan

The owner of the hotel hurried over to
their table.
'I am sorry,' he said to Gemma's dad.
'I have a new waiter for you.
The other one – he is gone!'

He shrugged his shoulders.
'These boys from the mountains – they come,
they go! They are nothing!
Istvan! Come here, please!'

A young man came over from
the other side of the room.
He had a crisp, white shirt, and wild,
black hair.

'This is Istvan, your new waiter.'

He introduced him to Gemma's mum and dad,
and then turned to Gemma.
'And this lovely little girl is Gemma.'

Gemma cringed – she was not a little girl.

'Good evening, Gemma,' said Istvan,
and Gemma looked up
into the deepest, blackest, and saddest eyes
she had ever seen.

'What do you want to drink?'
His voice was low and flat.

'Orange juice, please,' she said.

'OK!' That was all he said.

He brought the orange juice,
and put it down in front of her.
As he leaned over the table,
she saw his long, slim hands,
dark against his white shirt.

Perhaps Kloppos is not so boring after all
thought Gemma.

Istvan was very good.
He brought their meals quickly,
he didn't spill anything,
and he cleared up at once.

But he hardly ever spoke,
apart from 'Yes!' or 'No!'
in the same low, flat voice.

And he never, ever smiled.
Not once!
Even though Gemma smiled, and smiled
and smiled at him.

'What's up with our Gemma?' said her mum.
'She's not normally like this.'
'It's that Istvan,' said her dad,
'She's taken a shine to him.'
'Well I hope she can get him to smile.
He's so grumpy,' said her mum.
'He is not!' said Gemma angrily.
'See what I mean,' said her dad.

But her mum was right –
nothing that anyone said or did
could made Istvan smile
or lift the sadness from his eyes.

3 What Gemma Thought

Over the next few days,
Gemma thought more and more about Istvan.

As she was sunbathing
she thought about those dark eyes.
As she was buying postcards
she thought about that wild, black hair.
And as she swam among the rocks
she thought about those long, beautiful hands.

She started taking a real interest in meals.
She would arrive early,
and ask Istvan what she should have.

'What's the fish like?' she would say brightly.
'What are kebabs?'
'What's in the salad?'

And Istvan would say, 'It is good,'
or 'Tomato,' or 'OK!'
and that was it.
Nothing else!
And he never, ever smiled!

'I've never known Gemma like this,'
said her mum.
She was right.
Normally Gemma hardly touched her food,
let alone asked questions about it.

Gemma had her own tiny room next to
her mum and dad,
wtih a bathroom and a balcony
overlooking the beach.
The beach was small
with rocks running down into the sea
on either side.

In the evenings she would sit on the balcony
thinking about Istvan.

Why did he look so sad?
Why was he so unhappy?

It must be a broken heart!

It must be that he had loved some girl,
and she had rejected him,
and now he couldn't talk about it.

Gemma had read in a magazine
that boys found it difficult to talk
about things, to show their feelings.
They bottled things up,
and that made it worse.

The magazine said
that girls were good at talking about things,
and that they could help boys.
The magazine said
that if a girl really loved a boy,
she could help him express his feelings,
and take his pain away.

'That's it!' decided Gemma.
'He's got a broken heart,
and he won't talk about it.
He needs a girl to love him,
and help him express his feelings!'

Gemma knew exactly who that girl should be!

She could help him!
If only he would let her,
she could take the sadness out of those eyes.
If only he would turn to her,
she could make him smile again.

And then he would take her in his arms.
'Oh, my beautiful Gemma,'
he would say looking deep into her eyes,
'you have made my life worth living,
you have made me believe again.
Only you could have done this.'

And then he would hold her close,
and closer . . .
and then . . .!

4 What Gemma Did

Usually after their dinner,
Gemma and her mum and dad would walk
into the town to look at the shops.

One evening Gemma said,
'You go by yourselves.
I'm going to stay in and write
a few postcards.'

'Are you sure, love?' said her mum.
'All right then.'
And they went off.

Gemma waited in the dining-room
as one by one the tables emptied.
When Istvan came to clear away,
she was the only one left.

When he saw her there he stopped.
'I'll wait,' he said, and turned away.

'No, it's all right,' said Gemma.
'I've finished.'

He turned back.
'OK,' he said,
and started to clear away.

Gemma waited for a moment or two,
watching the quick movements of his hands
and wrists as he loaded the tray.

Then she said, 'Istvan?'
He looked up. 'You want something?'
'No, thank you. I don't want anything.'
He looked puzzled.

'Istvan?'
'Yes?'
'Istvan, why do you never smile?'
'What?'
'Smile, why do you never smile?'
'Oh, smile.'
He carried on clearing.
'What is there to smile for?'

'Oh, there must be lots of things.
Kloppos for a start.
Lots of people come here.
It's very popular.'

'Kloppos is not my place,' he said quickly.
'I do not come from Kloppos.'

'Where do you come from then?'

'From the mountains.
I come from the mountains.'

'Didn't you like it there?'
'Like it?'
'Yes!
Do you like it better here?
Is that why you came here?'

'No! . . . No!
I do not like it better here.
I like the mountains.'

This is impossible, thought Gemma.
He won't talk about anything!
He needs bringing out.
She tried again.

'I expect the mountains are very beautiful.'

'Beautiful?'

'Yes! The mountains! Beautiful!'
Why did he have to repeat everything?
'Oh, beautiful,' said Istvan.
'Yes, they are beautiful.
Very beautiful.'
His voice sounded bitter.

'And peaceful and quiet.
I'm sure there's lots of
peace and quiet there.'

'Peace ... ?'
He was wiping the table.
His hands slowed right down.
'Peace ... ?
Quiet ... ?'
His voice sunk.
'No ...
there is no ... peace ...
in the mountains ...
or quiet.'

'Well, what about your girlfriend?'

Istvan stopped completely.
'Girlfriend?' he said.
His hand trembled a little.

'Yes! Girlfriend.
I'm sure you must have a girlfriend.'

Istvan stared at the table.
He did not look at Gemma.
'No!' he said after a moment,
'I have no girlfriend.'

'Why not?
Did you have a girlfriend?
And did she break your heart?
Is that why you're so unhappy!'

He still hadn't moved.
'Please do not ask about these things,' he said.
His voice was a whisper.

I was right, thought Gemma.
He is heart-broken.
And he can't talk about it.
The magazine was right.
He needs to talk about it.
He needs me to help him talk about it.

'You can tell me, Istvan.
You can tell me all about your girlfriend.
If it would help.'

His fist was clenched.
He was breathing heavily.
'Please, no! Do not ask!' he said again.

He started rocking backwards and forwards,
backwards and forwards.

He's bottling it up, thought Gemma.
He won't let it out.
He must let it out!
'Let it out, Istvan,' she said gently.
'Tell me.'

'Please . . .' he said again.
He sounded desperate, his voice strangled.

'Don't keep it in, Istvan.
If you are in pain, then tell me.
Tell me what happened.
Perhaps I can help.
Tell me about your girlfriend.
Tell me . . .
OH!'

Istvan swept everything off the table
in one shattering crash,
and then stood before her,
his eyes blazing
and his face torn in agony.

'All right! I tell you! I tell you.
A girlfriend you say.
Yes, I had a girlfriend.
Yes! Katya was her name.
Yes! She was beautiful,
like the mountains, wild and free.
And I loved her.
Yes! I loved her.
And I tell you what happened.
One day they come for her.
In the village.
The soldiers.
They come for her.
And they take her from me.
From my arms.
And they laugh in my face.
They spit at me.
And there in the square,
in front of me,
and her mother,
they take her . . .
and they . . .
they . . .
they shoot her!'

He clutched his head in his hands, and howled.
'They shoot her! They shoot her!'
He pulled his hands away from his face,
and stared at Gemma.

'You little English girl.
What do you know?
You know nothing!
You come here in your plane,
with your questions,
and you talk of beautiful mountains,
and girlfriends,
and you know nothing!'
He was shouting in her face.

'You hear me, little English girl!
You know nothing!
Nothing!'

He turned,
and rushed from the room
crashing through tables and chairs.
At the last moment he looked back at Gemma.
'Nothing!' he shouted,
'You know nothing!'
And then he was gone.

Gemma pushed her chair away,
and stumbled through the dining-room
with her hand over her mouth.
She found her way into her bathroom.

And then she was horribly sick.

5 Gemma in her Room

Gemma lay with her head hung over the toilet.
When she stopped retching she started crying,
great heaving sobs that wrenched out of her.

His voice still rang in her ears,
'Nothing! You know nothing!'

When she was able,
she sat on the side of the bath
and tried to calm herself.

She tried to think of home,
of her mum and dad,
of school,
but their picture wouldn't come.

All she could see was the village square,
and the soldiers,
and the sudden splash of bright,
red blood on white walls.

She had seen lots of killings on the TV.
But that was different.
That was the TV.
That wasn't real.
Not like this.
She looked down at her arms and hands.
Katya had had arms and hands like this.
She pulled at the flesh,
and felt the bone beneath it.
She stretched her fingers,
and watched the tendons flex.

Real flesh, real bones, real blood.
Just like Katya's!

She had to hold herself to stop herself
retching again.

Her mum and dad came back.
Her mum tapped on her door.
'All right, Gemma?'

'Yes, mum,' she managed to say.
'I'm having an early night.'
'Are you sure?'
'Yes, mum. I'm fine.'
'Well, night night then.'
'Night night!'
And her mum's footsteps faded away
from her door.

Gemma took a blanket,
wrapped it around herself,
and went outside to the balcony and sat down.

She was still shaking.
She felt lonely, sick and frightened,
like a child suddenly forced to grow up.

She remembered the silly questions
she kept asking.
Kept on asking.
'Tell me!' she had said. 'Tell me!'

Istvan was right.
She was a little English girl who
knew nothing.
She tried to remember what she
had heard on the news, but it was no good.
It hadn't seemed real them.
Now it seemed only too real,
and everything else seemed just childish.

And that was what she was.
A child!
A child who knew nothing!

Katya couldn't have been
much older than she was.
What was she like? wondered Gemma.
Wild and free, Istvan had said.
Like the mountains.
And he had loved her.

Nobody had loved Gemma!

What had Katya done?
It must have been something brave,
thought Gemma.

What had Gemma done?
Watched TV!

It was not quite dark.
She looked out at the blackening sea,
still feeling sick and empty.

And then her eye was suddenly taken
by something down at the edge of the rocks.
Something white.
As if someone was sitting there
staring out at sea.
Someone in a white shirt.

Gemma watched for a moment,
and then quickly slid off her chair,
went through her room,
and opened the door.

She crept quietly along
to her mum and dad's room,
and listened at the door.
She could hear the television.
Soon they would go to bed.

Carefully she closed her door,
and then ran lightly along the corridor,
down the stairs,
past the desk,
and out into the cool night air.

6 On the Beach

There were a few people outside the hotel,
but the beach was deserted.

Gemma ran quickly over the warm sand
to the rocks.

He was still there,
sitting with his knees drawn up
under his chin.
She came up quietly behind him.
'Istvan?' she said. 'Istvan?'

For a moment he did not move,
and then very slowly,
as if he were coming back from a long way off,
he turned and looked at her.

'Oh, little English girl. It is you.'
'Istvan, I'm sorry.'

'No ... no ... it is I who am sorry,
I was unhappy.
I shouted.
I should not.'

'I didn't know.
You were right.
I know nothing.'

'No, no!
How should you know?
It is not your country.'

'But I should know.
I want to know.
Will you tell me about it?'

He looked at her in surprise.
'Tell you about it?'
'Yes, please.'

'You really want to know?'
'Yes, I really want to know.'

And so he did.
He turned his face to the sea, and spoke.
And she listened.

He told her of the mountains,
and of the forests,
and of the meadows of wild flowers.

He told her of the people, fierce and proud,
and of the villages and the herds of goats,
and of the little white churches
with guns hidden under the altars.

He told her of the soldiers
with their green uniforms and helicopters,
and of the groups of fighters hiding
in the caves. Katya had been a messenger for
one of these groups.

And as he talked, so her home, and her school,
all seemed to fade in Gemma's mind,
and these mountains seemed more real to her
than anything she had ever known.

When he finished they sat for some time
just looking out at the sea.

Then Gemma asked, 'What will you do now?'
Istvan shrugged his shoulders.
'I must go away.
They will come for me soon.
Someone will tell them about the
hotel tonight.
Do not worry.
They will not harm you.'

'Where will you go?'
'I will go to another country.
There I will carry on the fight.'

While he was talking,
a thought came into Gemma's mind.
Her heart started beating quickly.

She sat very still, trying to calm herself,
and then said quietly,
'Why don't you come to my country?'

'To your country, little English girl?
Yes, that would be good.
But I cannot.
I do not have the papers.
They would not let me.'

Everything around Gemma seemed to pause.
The sky, the rocks, even the waves
seemed to be waiting.

'There is one way you could get in.'
'And what is that?'
'You could marry me!'
There was silence.
Istvan turned round slowly.
'What?
What is this you are saying,
little English girl? Marry you?'

'Yes!
If you marry me, you will have the papers.'

'What? You are serious?'

Gemma sat perfectly still.
She looked him steadily in the eye.
Her voice was firm.

'Yes! I am serious.'

He looked at her long and hard.
'Yes, you are serious.
But you know not what you say.
You are too young.'
'No, I am not,' lied Gemma. 'In my country
I am old enough.'

'And your father, your mother.
They would not allow this.'

'They would not know.
It would only be to get you into the country.'

Istvan nodded slowly.
'Yes. You would do this.
For me, Istvan, you would do this.'

'Yes! For you, Istvan, I would do this.'
He looked at her for a long time.
'It cannot be,' he said at last.
'You forget.
We keep your passport at the hotel.
I know you are not old enough.'

Gemma sagged.
She gave a little cry, and lowered her head.

'And now I must go.
But listen, little English girl.'

He leaned forward,
and lifted her up by the shoulders.

He smiled,
a rich, warm smile,
and there was no sadness in his eyes.

'I tell you this.
Never will I forget these words
you have spoken to me tonight.
I will keep them here in my heart forever.
And this thing I call you,
this little English girl,
it is not right.
You are a woman,
a grown woman, proud and beautiful.'

And then, very gently, he kissed her.

'And now I go.'

He turned,
and made his way quickly over the rocks.

Gemma watched the white shirt as it
moved here and there,
until it became a blur,
and then a shadow,
and then disappeared.

She turned,
and walked slowly back over the sand
to the hotel.

7 Afterwards

The next morning the owner of the hotel
served them breakfast himself.

'What's happened to Istvan?'
asked Gemma's mum.
'Where is he?'

'These boys from the mountains,'
said the owner.
'They come, they go!
They are nothing!'

A few days later a soldier came to the hotel.
He wanted to speak to Gemma.
He had a green uniform, dark glasses,
and a gun strapped to his hip.
He asked her what she knew of Istvan.

'Nothing,' she said, 'I know nothing!'

Where was he going?
Where had he been?
What did she know?

'Nothing,' she said again. 'I know nothing!'

He looked at her for a few moments,
and then shrugged his shoulders,
and went away.

The rest of the holiday came and went.
Gemma swam, and sunbathed,
and spent a long time walking
among the rocks.

'Our Gemma's very quiet,' said her dad.

'Just leave her,' said her mum.

And it was only when they left,
and they were in the plane,
and Gemma looked out of the window,
and saw the mountains falling away
beneath her – green with little white villages –
that the tears came –
great sobs that ran helplessly down her face,
and soaked her T-shirt.